The Intimate Art of the Little Paper Costume **KOKIGAMI** ▪

KOKIGAMI

The Intimate Art of the Little Paper Costume

Ten Speed Press

"Every creative act involves . . . a new innocence of perception, liberated from the cataract of accepted belief."
Arthur Koestler.

First published in The United States 1990
Text © 1990 Burton Silver
Artwork and paper sculpture © 1990
Heather Busch

TEN SPEED PRESS
P.O. Box 7123
Berkeley, California 94707

ISBN 0-89815-397-2

Library of Congress Catalog Card Number: 90-71176

Grateful thanks to the trustees for acccess to the Scott Sainsbury Collection.

Originated and devised by Heather Busch and Burton Silver.

Compiled by Silverculture Press,
487 Karaka Bay Road, Wellington 3,
New Zealand.

Book design and production by
Trevor Plaisted, Wellington.

Back cover photograph by Annelies Vanderpoel.

Printed in Hong Kong.

1 2 3 4 5 — 94 93 92 91 90

C ONTENTS

■

FOREWORD

■

okigami has fascinated me since 1974 when I was introduced to it by the delightful Dr. Itazura in Tokyo. One afternoon while discussing male sexual awareness in our respective cultures, Dr. Itazura mentioned that the art of the little paper costume was clear evidence of the Japanese male's ability to gain a deeper intellectual and emotional understanding of his libidinal urges. Naturally I asked him what this art was. Without replying he stood up and left the room, returning a moment later with an ornately carved sandalwood box which he carefully placed on the floor in front of me. Inside were a collection of colorful paper sculptures that looked for all the world like children's toys or Christmas tree decorations. When I suggested that this was what they were, he laughed and fetched a series of old scrolls which clearly showed just how wrong I was.

I had of course heard of the Nippon Slip-on and for that matter I was familiar with the expression Art Dicko, but had, like many other Westerners, assumed that these terms referred to the colorful and often ornate condoms favored by Japanese of high breeding. As a sexologist I prided myself with my knowledge of things erotic, but here before me was hard evidence of a most advanced sexual practice that clearly left the likes of the Karma Sutra for dead. This was not some sex manual that promoted a variety of interesting physical positions, but a most ingenious

method of heightening the enjoyment of the sex act by putting the participants in touch with their inner sexual fantasies. What could be more intriguing!

For the Japanese, the pleasures of the flesh are natural and normal, and sexual happiness has always been regarded as a basic human right. Given these attitudes and the advanced nature of their culture, it is not surprising that they developed a highly sophisticated method of increasing sexual enjoyment.

The male has always been dominant in Japanese society and from the earliest times ensured that his sexual needs were well catered by the availability of women trained in the art of lovemaking. Having taken this training to an extremely high level it was obvious to him, as it seems not to have been to other cultures, that any additional pleasure could only be found by somehow training his own sexual ability, the center of which was the phallus. This I believe was the guiding principle behind the evolution of Kokigami.

This beautifully simple system allows the mind to get more deeply in touch with the male sexual center by pretending that it is something else. By slipping a paper sculpture of an animal over his organ, the male is able to give it the qualities of that animal and relate to it on another level. It instantly becomes far more than a rather odd piece of blood-engorged flesh with a mind of its own. It is given a new personality, making the organ much easier to relate to and therefore to understand and control.

More importantly perhaps for us in the West is that Kokigami enables women to come to terms with the male organ and relate to it in a nonthreatening way. In a practice spanning more than thirty years I have found no better method of quickly demystifying the penis and dispelling its perceived power; no other simple technique that enables couples to overcome their inhibitions, get in touch with their guiding fantasies, and so move to more loving, understanding, and pleasurable sexual relations.

But you mustn't get the idea that Kokigami is all terribly serious and something that only sex therapists should use. On the contrary, its wonderfully simple techniques are based upon having a great deal of light-hearted fun, designed to relax and encourage intimacy.

Indeed the only problem with this art form is that Western males find it initially very difficult to accept. Unlike the more sensitive Japanese, his attitudes toward sex are almost exclusively physically based, so the notion of slipping something over his member that does not have some immediate physical function, like a condom, is totally foreign to him. This fixation with his physical sexuality renders him incapable of fully understanding his complete sensual self. At best he gets only half the picture, and finding it incomprehensible, begins to build up negative feelings. Sadly, these feelings lead to much of the frustration and violence which typifies many Western relationships. It is my firm belief that Kokigami can do a great deal to restore the much needed balance between the mental and physical, and I am sure this first introduction to this art form will go a long way towards achieving that.

There are no special tricks to this art of the little paper costume. No hours of practice, no tedious new vocabulary to learn. With this book and a pair of scissors, you can add a whole new dimension to your own and your partner's sexuality. Once you get past the absurd taboos that inhibit sexual expression and understanding in our society, you'll be able to use Kokigami to bring a new meaning and pleasure to your sensual world.

Dr. Mary Scrott

Dr. Mary Scrott

INTRODUCTION

■ *An Historical Perspective*

The origins of Kokigami have traditionally been the subject of spirited academic debate. On the one side are those who claim it has direct links with *origami*, the art of paper folding, while on the other are those who consider it owes its genesis to *kirigami*, or cut art. It seems likely however that it predated both of these paper art forms, as erotic prints (*shunga*) clearly show the little paper costume in use as early as the eighth century. In recent times there seems to be a general consensus amongst Oriental and Western scholars alike that kokigami probably evolved from the ancient Japanese art of *Tsutsumi* or packaging.

The word Tsutsumi comes from the verb Tsutsushimu, to refrain, to be discreet or moderate. The Japanese culture shuns the direct, the frank or blunt in favor of things which are indirect, controlled, and restrained. This ethic plays an important role in gift giving, where it is considered most discourteous to pass an unwrapped, unconcealed gift to another.

It was natural that in male-dominated Japanese society the gift that was perceived to be the most important of all, the giver of life, would be treated in the same manner. Indeed there is clear evidence from early literature that men of the upper classes wrapped their penises before retiring to the conjugal chamber. Several passages in the *Kojiki*, a book of legends dating from A.D. 712,

tell of men spending "much time with fine silks and ribbons." For the more complex he could make the wrapping, the longer his wife would take to unwrap "the present" and the more he would be rewarded by "the pleasure of the fingers undoing."

The Japanese love of ceremony formalized these "gift giving" sessions and infused them with a degree of restrained elegance which would be of great interest to us today had the practice continued. The reasons why it ceased completely are unclear, but there can be no doubt it was the forerunner of Kokigami as we know it today.

The switch in emphasis from the purely physical pleasures enjoyed in the old tsutsumi ceremony to a concentration on heightened satisfaction through mental control, as practiced in Kokigami, came about with the arrival of Buddhism in the sixth century. The deeply held Shinto beliefs in the divinity of the phallus were not wiped out by Buddhism, but rather absorbed by it, and modified. It seems likely that many aspects of Kokigami as it was practiced from the eighth century on were developed by Shinto priests. Strongly influenced by Buddhism, they sought ways of transcending the physical center of their being by exploring it in greater depth, trying to get in touch with it in much the same way an actor gets in touch with his character.

Indeed the similarity of these methods and those used in Japanese noh theater are often noted when reference is made to the derivation of the word Kokigami. *Gami* is the word for paper, and a *koki* is a small piece of cloth worn at the waist by the supporting actors (*waki*) in noh theater. All the actors in noh are male, and they use the koki in a variety of ways to make quick character changes. It can be used as a hat, a blindfold, a mask, even a weapon. While it is highly unlikely that koki were ever used to cover the male organ during a performance, their function as dramatic changers of character fits well with the concepts of Kokigami.

By the middle of the Heian period (794-1185), Japan's great golden era of artistic development, Kokigami had become firmly established as a path to sensual enlightenment amongst the aristocratic classes. But it was not until the late eighteenth century, when the price of paper fell, that it ceased to be the exclusive preserve of the rich and became popular with all strata of Japanese society. In recent years Kokigami has attracted a lot of interest from psychotherapists in America and it seems likely that this ancient art will soon enjoy a new popularity in the West.

彼女のお呼びに応えて鴨がおでましになったものの
広い空を見たからには羽ばたきたくなっちゃったかも

The Goose was a popular koki in eighteenth-century Japan.

GETTING STARTED

遊び好きなお魚ちゃんがまた碧け目に入りたがっているわ
イカはイカで感じやすい足を咥えてやっと見つけた獲物を
逃すまいと必死でがんばっているの

"Lovers at Play" from an early nineteenth-century print.

Most Western men react to Kokigami with a mixture of disbelief, embarrassment, and indignation. Surely no male would consider twirling about in front of his lover with a paper fish slipped over his most intimate organ. And making cheeky bubble sounds through protruding lips at the same time? You can't be serious! It's a natural reaction that rises mainly from a lack of knowledge about the gentle and restrained way in which this ancient art is approached.

In Japan, Kokigami is practiced with a great deal of subtlety and refinement that minimizes any initial social discomfort. While some men may feel relaxed about wearing a koki straight away, most will benefit from the more oblique traditional methods of introduction, which are based on a delightful blend of intimacy, surprise, and humor.

A good way of getting started is to gift wrap the book and hide it under your partner's pillow. This will enable you to share it together in an intimate and supportive setting. Study the pictures carefully and ask each other which you most like and dislike. Which koki do you think would be most appropriate for him to wear? Which ones can you imagine your friends or your father wearing? When making your choice of which koki to begin with, don't forget that the partner will be required to play a complimentary character. For many couples these first discussions can be most revealing and quickly lead to a deeper understanding of one's own and each other's unique erotic personalities.

Under each picture you will find the script, or *serifu*, which is divided up into the Character, the Call, the Reply, and the Play. While they are only

■ *Choosing a Koki*

紙初体験

intended as suggestions, reading them out to each other should help you to clarify your feelings about them and get you in the mood to start. You will notice that the serifu, in most cases translated directly from the Japanese, are rich with sexual imagery and the double entendre. This is quite traditional and is done in order to provoke discussion and provide a certain degree of levity which relaxes the participants.

However, they are only intended as a guide to get you started and need not be followed to the letter. Indeed, it has always been assumed that couples will make up their own, much longer dialogues, into which they can weave information of a more personal nature.

Now is a good time to discuss what will happen in your Play. What will you say and do, and how will it end? Remember, innovation is the key with Kokigami. The more avenues that can be explored, the more barriers will be broken down, and the more pleasures that can be enjoyed.

Before cutting out the first koki, it's a good idea to help your partner check his size, using the sizing diagram, or *kata*, on page 17. Many men in the West are sensitive about their size, so he may be a little reluctant at first to reveal his dimensions. If your man is small in that department it's important to reassure him by downplaying the

importance of size. It may also help to point out that with Kokigami you are only interested in the width and not the length.

Once you have made your koki it's important that it be presented subtly before actually being worn. In Japan, koki were traditionally placed so as to just peep suggestively out of the little drawer at the bottom of the pillow box. Nowadays nobody uses pillow boxes, and koki are placed in an intriguing variety of places designed to surprise and excite: on the bedroom door handle, as part of an ikebana arrangement (see back cover), in a little nest made out of sheet folds — the possibilities are endless. But remember, the position you choose should be appropriate to the character of the koki. For example you might hide the Dragon in a cave of bedclothes and let your partner find it with a flashlight.

In order to help overcome any initial embarrassment that may be felt when wearing a koki, it is helpful to begin with a very low light. (The use of candles while wearing paper koki is not advisable). Music, too, is useful in setting a relaxed mood and, if in character with the koki, will greatly enhance the experience. You may like to play the sound track from a TV series like "The Untouchables" or "Naked City" when wearing the Private Investigator. "The Yellow Rose of Texas" would go well with the Rose, "Fly Me To The Moon" for the Space Shuttle, "Chattanooga Choo Choo" with the Steam Engine, and Peter, Paul, and Mary's "Car, Car" or "Puff the Magic Dragon" are just a few examples of songs that could provide the right atmosphere and give him something to move in time with.

Some men like to put their koki on themselves and surprise their lovers, but many find their partner's involvement in this delicate stage helps overcome any initial awkwardness. Touch and stroke the koki as if it were real. Talk and sing to it, play with it, become totally familiar with it before you slip it on, and once it is on, keep up the dialogue.

In order to explore the deep character of each koki the Japanese do a very effective exercise called *Renso Gehmu*, which you may like to try. The koki is put on without the partner looking and covered with a little cloth or tissue. The wearer then makes noises and movements appropriate to his character while his partner tries to guess which one he is wearing. (With over six hundred different koki currently available in Japan, this can be a daunting task.) In order to keep his partner from guessing, the wearer adopts the most subtle, minimalist forms of character expression.

Many couples enjoy personalizing their koki by decorating them with things like wool, feathers, leaves, sequins, or glitter, and they often spray them with their favorite perfumes. Luminous paint is also well worth a try. It makes for a most exciting display with all the lights turned off.

As Kokigami becomes a regular part of your sexual lifestyle, you will find new areas of exploration occur quite naturally. Trying unusual settings, working at co-operative and multi-koki wearing, and experiencing the interesting complexities of advanced group play are just a few of the delights that await you on your journey into the inner depths of your sensual self.

# INSTRUCTIONS

ead all the instructions through carefully before you start. You will need a sharp pair of scissors for cutting the outside edge, a sharp blade for making the slots and for fine cutting, round pencil or pen for stretching the paper, plus nimble fingers and lots of time and desire.

Cutting and Construction:

Remember to check your personal size by using the sizing diagram on page 17 before you begin. This will ensure a firm and comfortable fit. Only cut the slits that relate to your size so as not to weaken the tabs with too many cuts.

When cutting, follow the solid black lines around the edge of each piece of the pattern. Black lines also indicate slots which will need to be cut with the blade. Take care to find all the slots as there are usually quite a few and they are sometimes hard to find. They all need to be cut out on a flat surface before the construction process begins.

Dotted lines indicate folds, and you will need to check whether they should be made into a hill or a valley. You can do this by referring to the picture of the completed koki.

Folding:

Special folding is sometimes necessary to give extra rigidity and strength. The most dramatic example of this is the Fire Engine's long extension ladder. To make it stiff and strong, the edge of the ladder is folded. The running board along the edge of the Fire Engine also uses this technique, as do the other vehicles, to hold its shape.

Stretching:

This process is used to twist or curl the paper. Using the side of a pencil, pull the paper firmly between your thumb and the pencil. Repeat until the paper falls into a natural curl. Take care not to pull too hard and rip the paper. This technique is used in shaping the Squid's tentacles, the fringe of the Horse, the tail feathers of the Cock, and to a lesser extent on the Moth's and Dragon's feelers. It is also used to shape the front bumper of the Sports Car, the feelers of the Fish, the hairy tips of the Pig's ears and the Dog's ears.

Interlocking:

The koki are held together by means of tags and slots. No glue or tape is normally required, though some taping may be advisable after frequent vigorous use.

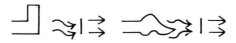

These tags have to be eased and wriggled in sideways, then straightened in line with the slot.

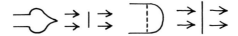

These are less secure so once through they should be bent over.

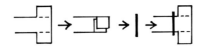

These tags are very secure. They are folded small to fit through the slot, then unfolded once in place.

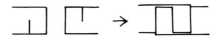

These lock together, slot to slot, and lie flat to form one continuous band. They are mostly used to attach the koki to the penis.

Construction:

Once it is cut, folded, and stretched, construct the koki by following the alphabet. For example, A goes to A1, then A2 goes to A3, and so on, depending on how many steps are needed to attach and position each piece of the pattern. The next piece will be B, which will go to B1 and so on.

Order of Difficulty:

Like origami, Kokigami is a very old paper art that has been refined over the centuries to enable its practice with a minimum of skill. Even so, it is a good idea to begin with the easiest patterns first. The most basic ones are the Moth and then the Rose. The Dog, Squid, Private Investigator, Fire Engine, Dragon, Fish, and Sports Car are a little more difficult. The most advanced are the Cock, Horse, Space Shuttle, Pig, and lastly the Steam Engine.

DOG: LEAD ATTACHMENT.

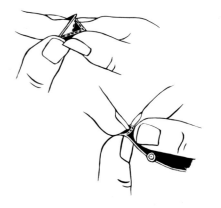

FIRE ENGINE: ATTACHING THE EXTENSION LADDER.

COCK: SHAPING THE BEAK.

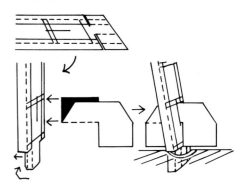

How to Measure Your Size

It is important to take care with the sizing to ensure your koki fits firmly and doesn't fall off during The Play. This can be embarrassing and inhibit the natural flow of action and dialogue.

When sizing, the organ should be rigid and pressed down firmly onto this page. As this creates a rather difficult viewing angle, it is a good idea to get your partner to check your reading.

Measure the size at the thickest part (usually the stem) by looking down directly over the top of the organ or by using a flat surface laid along its side. Having found your width (e.g., B+, C, etc), you can cut out the two corresponding slits marked on the holding tabs and be assured of a good fit. Remember to cut only the slits for your size so as not to weaken the tabs with too many cuts.

A   B   C

A+ B+
B− C−

Sizing

17

Ryu
紙茎

 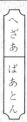

RYU : THE DRAGON

The crafty Dragon likes to breathe his fire into the dark jeweled cave. Ravaging, vengeful, sly.

———

THE CALL: *"Where are my precious jewels? My treasures? My trophies? Are they hidden there in your dark cave?"*

THE REPLY: *"Come on hot stuff! Careful the iron gates don't snap shut and sever your burning tongue!"*

THE PLAY: *With arms outstretched and fingers curled like claws, move forward warily with the knees bent. The hips may be flicked about spasmodically accompanied by the low seductive roar of a raging furnace.*

19

22

へざあ　ばあとん

ONDORI : THE COCK

The haughty cock puffs himself up and crows arrogantly from the roof top. Inflated, vain, jubilant.

THE CALL: "Cock-a-doodle-doo!"

THE REPLY: "Get lost feather brain!"

THE PLAY: Strut about stiffly with hands on hips and the head held high. Crow loudly infront of your partner, but then move closer and make exciting little clucking sounds.

へざあ　ばあとん

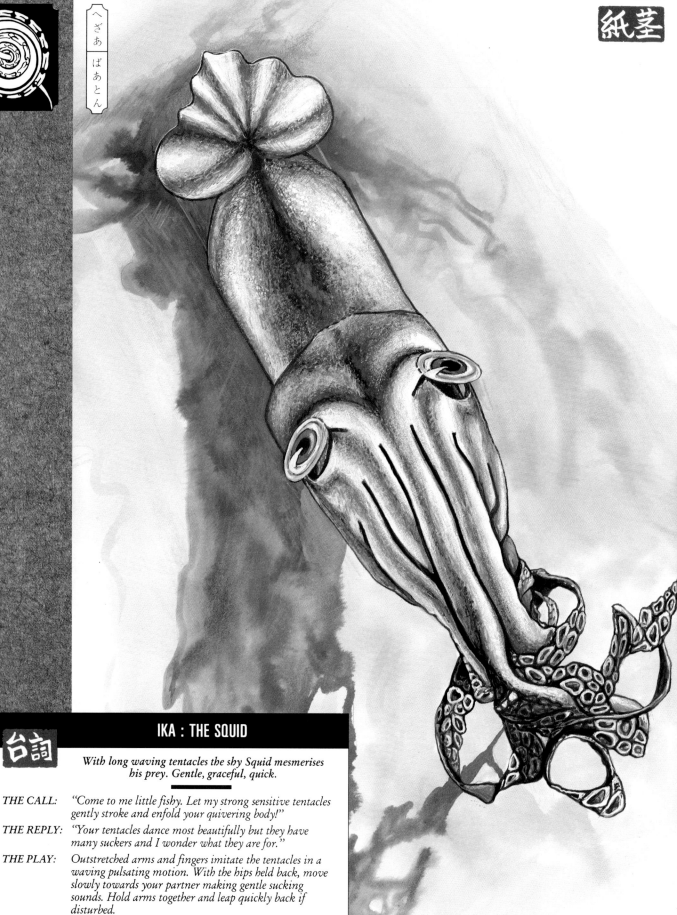

台詞

IKA : THE SQUID

*With long waving tentacles the shy Squid mesmerises
his prey. Gentle, graceful, quick.*

THE CALL: *"Come to me little fishy. Let my strong sensitive tentacles
gently stroke and enfold your quivering body!"*

THE REPLY: *"Your tentacles dance most beautifully but they have
many suckers and I wonder what they are for."*

THE PLAY: *Outstretched arms and fingers imitate the tentacles in a
waving pulsating motion. With the hips held back, move
slowly towards your partner making gentle sucking
sounds. Hold arms together and leap quickly back if
disturbed.*

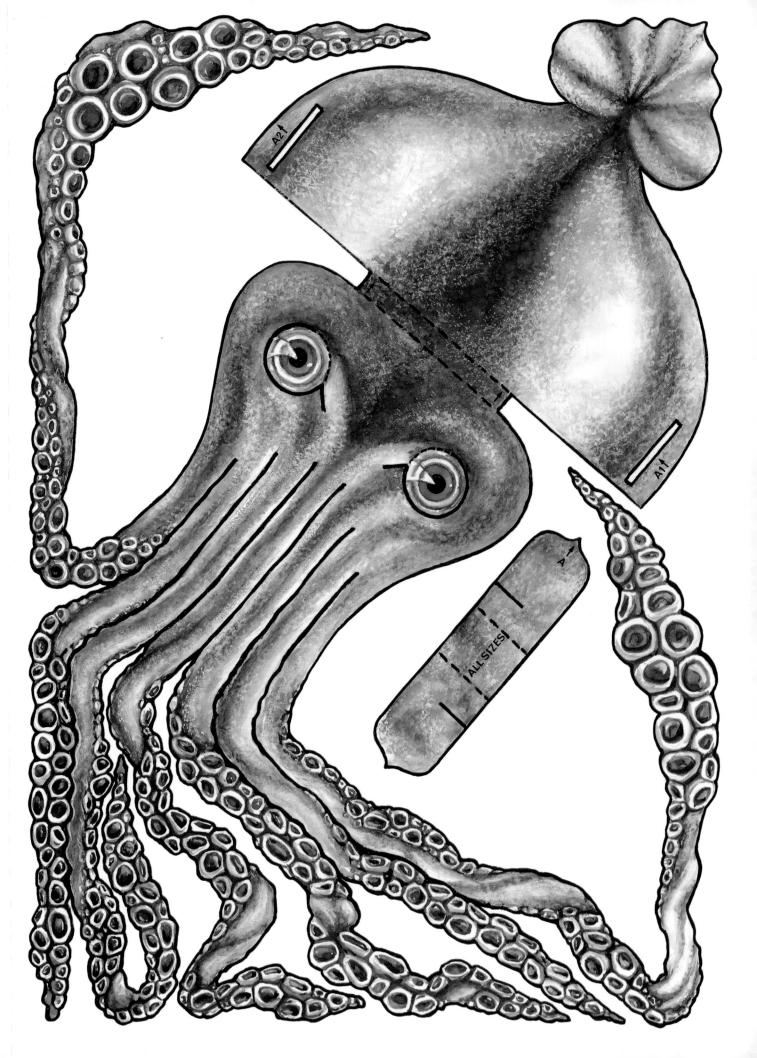

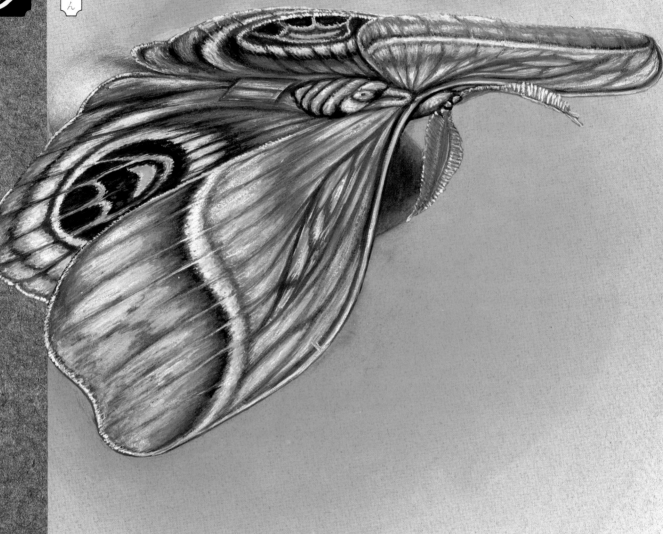

GA : THE MOTH

Fluttering silently on silken wings the Moth is hopelessly intoxicated by the light. Soft, vulnerable, tender.

THE CALL: *"I am dazzled by your brightness. Let me bathe in the glow of your sparkling radiance."*

THE REPLY: *"Hotter and hotter burns my glistening light! Beware you do not singe your beautiful silken wings."*

THE PLAY: *Stand on tiptoes and take precise little steps, twirling around your partner with arms and fingers fluttering in a wing-like manner. Allow the lips, head, and hips to tremble slightly.*

へ ざ あ
ば あ と ん

BUTA : THE PIG

*The happy Pig likes to root about in the soft earth
with his pink nose. Eager, expectant, watchful.*

THE CALL: *"Oink! Oink! How about a bit of juicy swill?"*

THE REPLY: *"Here Piggy Wiggy! Lots of lovely warm slops just for
you!"*

THE PLAY: *Thrust the hips forward and up with short jerky
movements while jumping quickly towards your partner.
Make low, enticing grunts. If thwarted, jump back and
emit a startled squeal.*

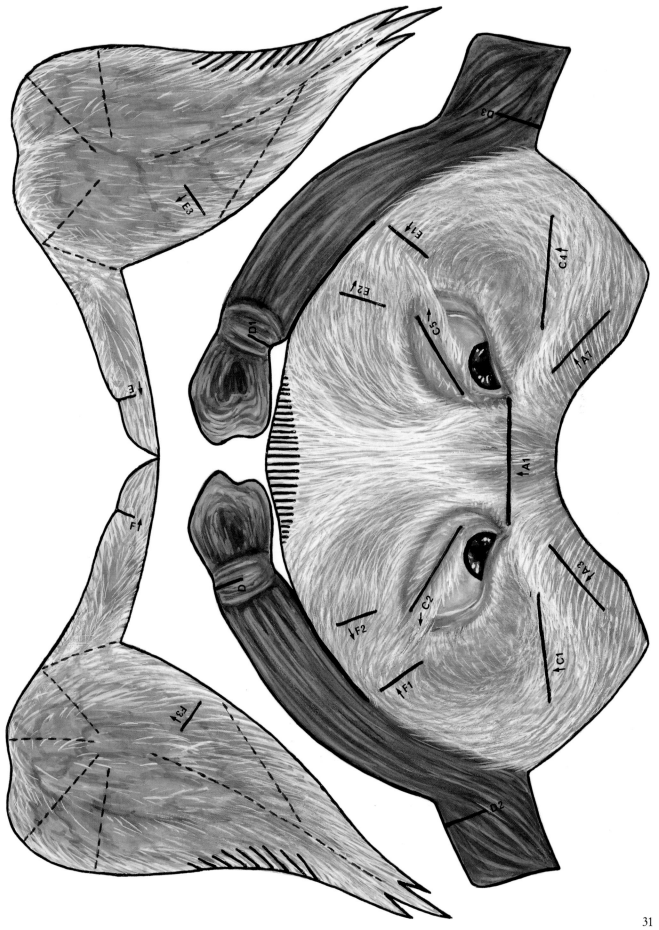

31

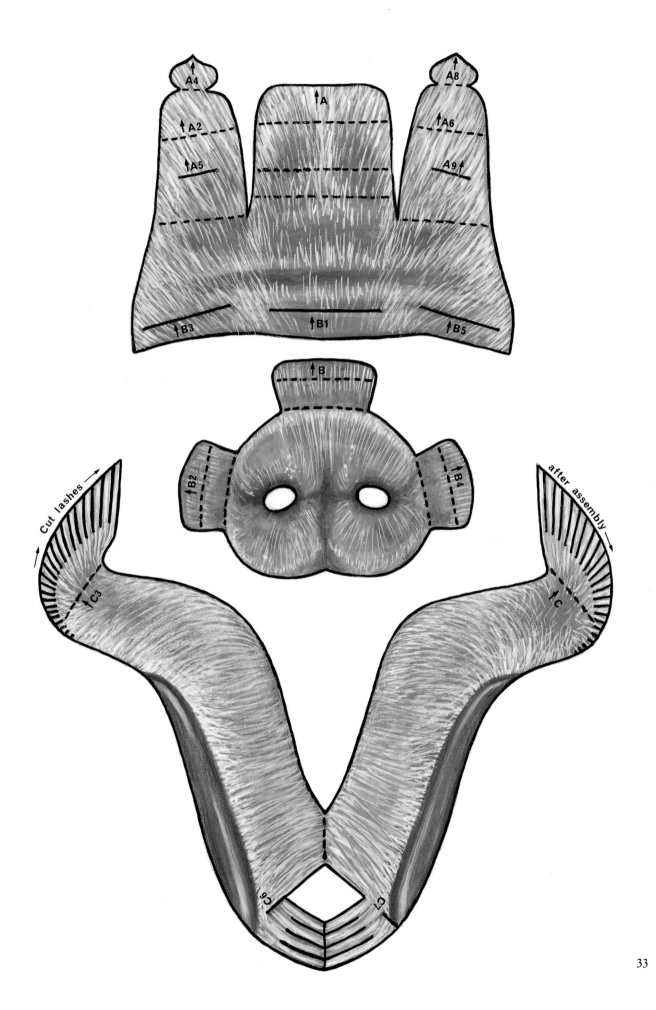

33

へ ざ あ
ば あ と ん

SAKANA : THE FISH

*The playful Fish likes to wriggle through the weeds
and dart into crevices. Fun-loving, alert, sleek.*

THE CALL: *"Hey little sea anemone, your tiny red tentacles can't
catch me!"*

THE REPLY: *"Can't they just! Let's wait and see!"*

THE PLAY: *With arms held out from the body to simulate fins, dart
enticingly about in front of your partner making cheeky
bubble sounds through protruding lips.*

へざあ｜ばあとん

UMA : THE HORSE

*With flared nostrils and flowing mane the mighty Horse
gallops into the forest. Strong, noble, free.*

THE CALL: *"Where are my oats? Where is my straw?"*

THE REPLY: *"Your oats are ready, the straw is warm and my stable
door is open, but you still have a long way to go!"*

THE PLAY: *With reins held firmly in both hands, raise the knees high
and gallop towards your partner. The rider may call out,
"Whoa! Easy boy!" and pull back on the reins while at the
same time thrusting the hips forward violently.*

39

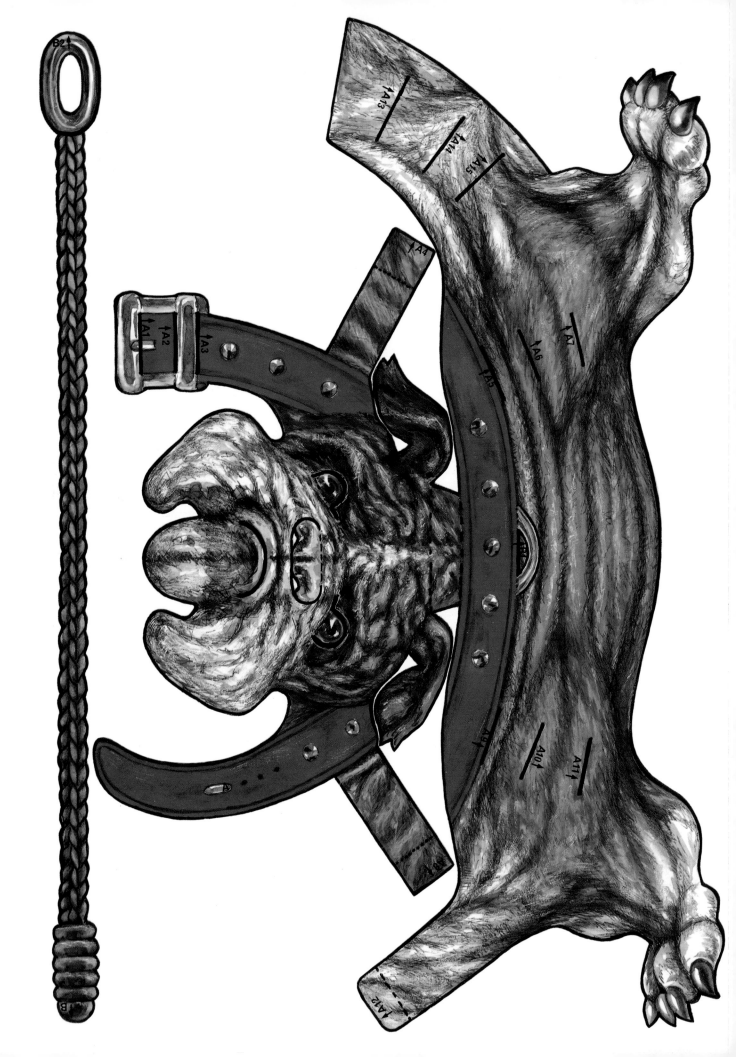

INU : THE DOG

The muscle-bound Dog strains at his leash pulling his master off balance. Slobbery, powerful, disobedient.

THE CALL: *"Ruff! Ruff! Let me get at that pussy cat!"*

THE REPLY: *"Meow!"*

THE PLAY: *One hand grasps the leash attempting to restrain the dog while at the same time the hips are thrust vigorously forward and back to simulate his attempts at freedom. The master may shout, "Sit!" "Lie down!" or "Get in behind!"*

へ ざ あ
ば あ と ん

台詞 BARA : THE ROSE

In full bloom, the delicate Rose unfolds its velvet petals.
Fragrance abounds. Vibrant, aromatic, thorny.

THE CALL: *"Come fuzzy bee and taste my pearly nectar! Feel my soft petals against your tiny cheeks!"*

THE REPLY: *"Buzzzzz, hold still sweet-scented beauty and let my long tongue probe your honey hole."*

THE PLAY: *The feet are held together and the body stretched upwards like the main stem. Then the forearms are extended out like other stems and the hands become more blooms quivering seductively in the breeze.*

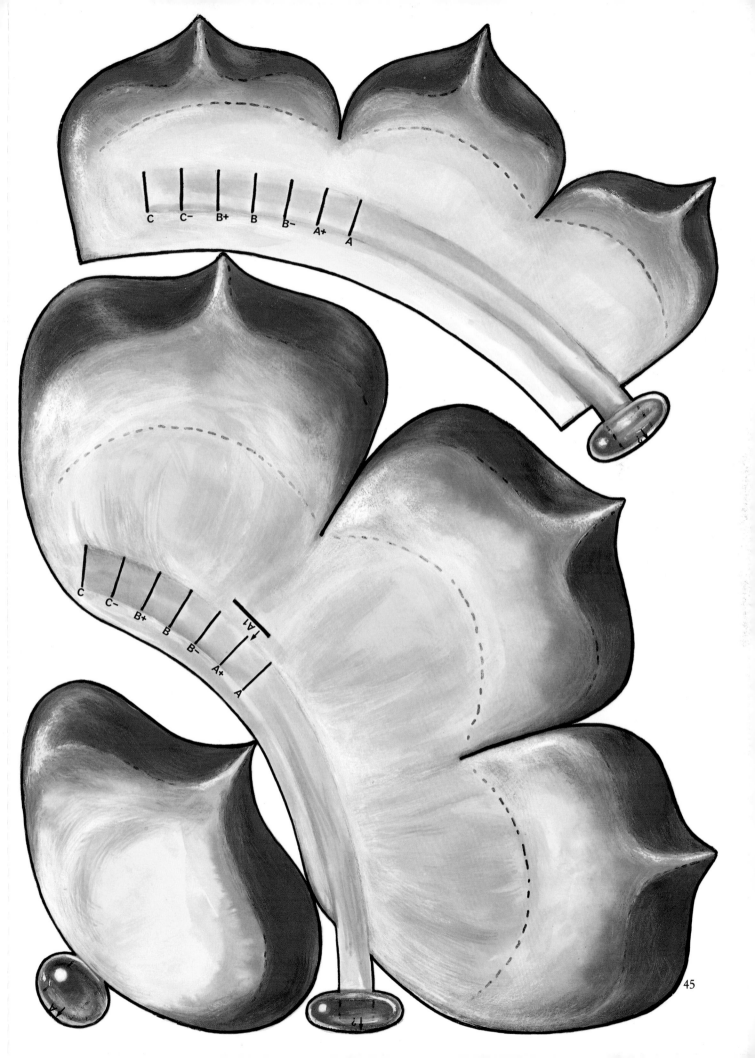

KURUMA : THE SPORTS CAR

The Sports Car speeds along narrow country lanes, squealing noisily as it accelerates round corners. Fast, exciting, flashy.

THE CALL: *"Rrrrrrmmmmm! Beep! Beep! Hey can you give me a hand to park this thing?"*

THE REPLY: *Left hand down a bit, bit more.....Plenty of room on this side....Steady....Whoa! That's far enough!"*

THE PLAY: *One hand is held in front gripping the steering wheel while the other changes gear. The hips are thrust forward and the shoulders back, make deep throbbing exhaust noises.*

KISHA : THE STEAM ENGINE

With smoke belching and cinders flying the big Steam Engine roars out of the tunnel. Proud, throbbing, hot.

THE CALL: *"Chuff chuff chuff chuff, chuff chuff chuff chuff, Whooooooooooooooooo! Got to make it! Got to make it!"*

THE REPLY: *"Please stand well clear of the tracks, the 11:25 express is coming through!"*

THE PLAY: *Swing forearms vertically to simulate pistons. Move toward your partner in a straight line while making loud, rhythmic steam emission noises. Blow whistle before moving off again.*

51

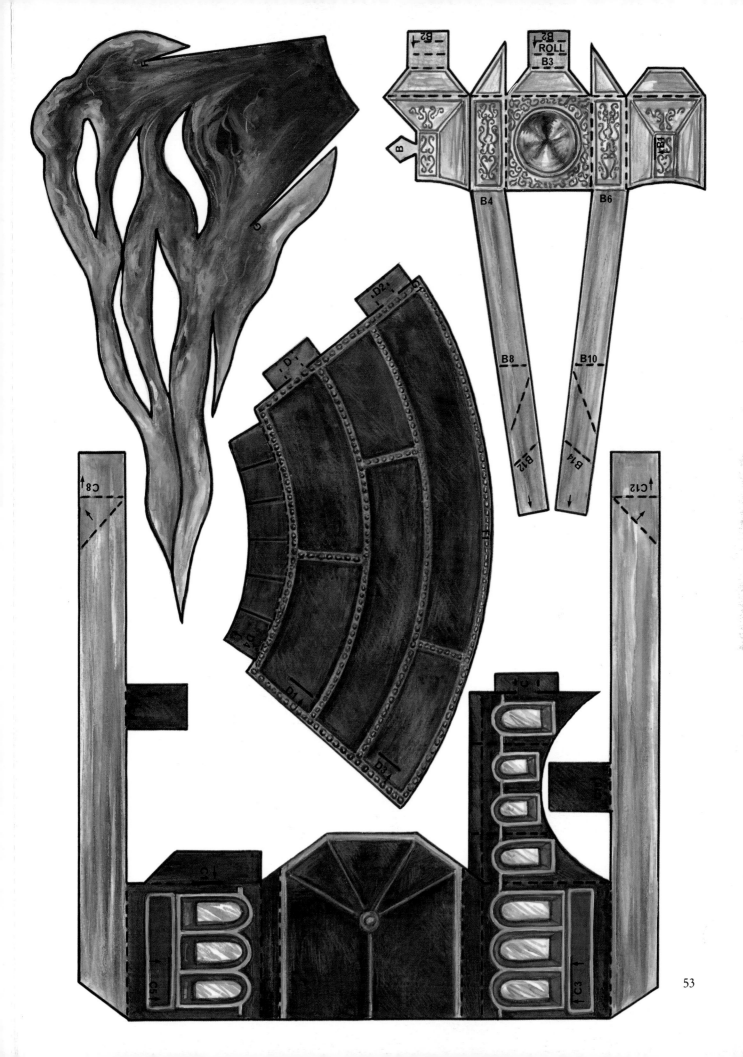

53

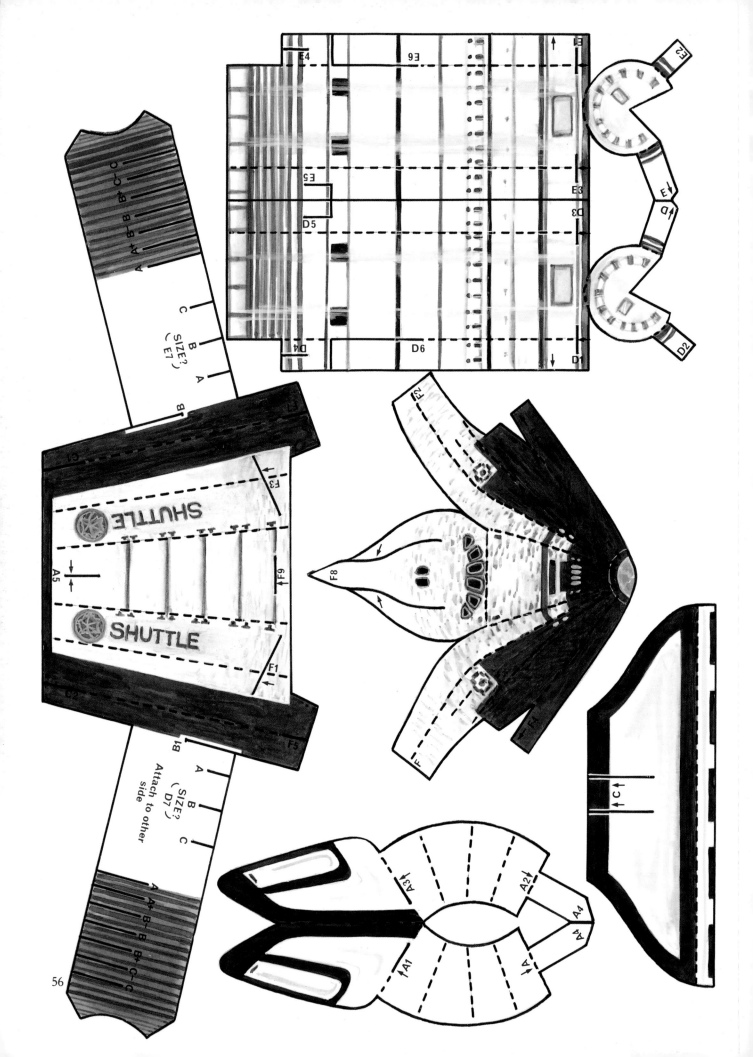

SHUTTLE

SHUTTLE

SIZE?
(E7)

SIZE?
(D7)

Attach to other side

56

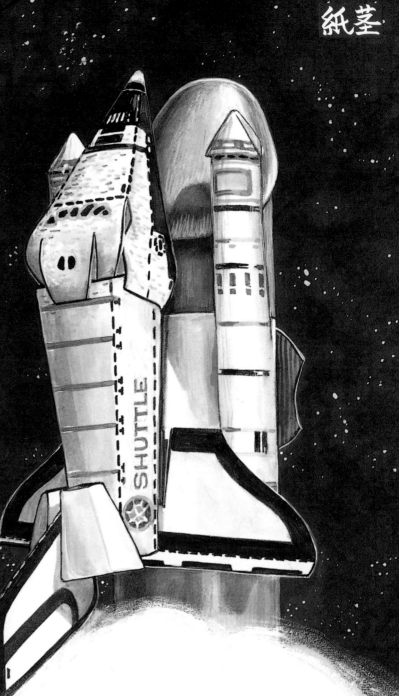

SUPEHSU SHATORU : THE SPACE SHUTTLE

The Space Shuttle waits for the mighty rocket to carry it into the black silence of space. Rigid, swift, exploratory.

THE CALL: *"5...4...3...2...1...We have lift-off!"*

THE REPLY: *"This is Venus Base Station. Prepare for docking."*

THE PLAY: *Hold arms out from the body like delta wings, lean well forward and rush towards your partner making loud wooshing sounds. Later, swirl around silently as you go into orbit and prepare for re-entry.*

へざあ　ばあとん

SHOBOSHA : THE FIRE ENGINE

台詞

With lights flashing and siren wailing the Fire Engine speeds towards the big fire. Urgent, important, gushing.

THE CALL: *"Weeeeeooooo! Clear the way! Put up the ladder! Turn on the hose!"*

THE REPLY: *"Oh put me out! Put me out!"*

THE PLAY: *Hold one hand on top of the head and open and close it to simulate the flashing light. With the other hand pretend to hold the steering wheel and rush round your partner in ever decreasing circles. On reaching "the fire" put up the ladder.*

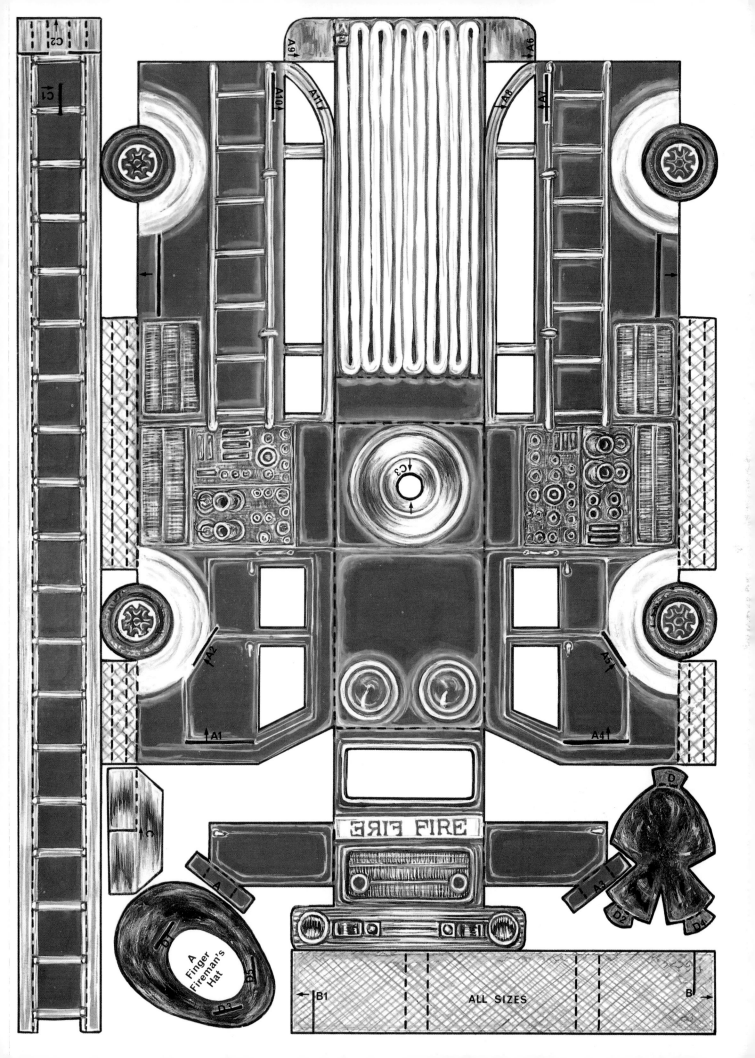

FIRE

A Finger Fireman's Hat

ALL SIZES

へざあ ばあとん

SHIRITSU TANTEI : THE PRIVATE INVESTIGATOR

台詞

*Ever watchful, the Private Dick lurks just out of sight,
always ready for action. Cool, calm, tough.*

THE CALL: *"If you want a quick solution we're going to have to
move fast!"*

THE REPLY: *"That's fine by me. You got any clues?"*

THE PLAY: *With shoulders hunched and hands deep in pockets,
saunter forward. If things get tricky shoot first and ask
questions later.*

63

■ *B i o g r a p h i c a l   N o t e s*

Heather Busch and Burton Silver are New Zealanders who share a unique vision engendered by that country's remote geographical location and its sensuous landscape. They arrived at their intense interest in Kokigami by very separate paths, one biological and the other spiritual, each representing the twin aspects of this special art.

Burton Silver is well known for his conservation work with hedgehogs and especially for the very successful "Hedgehog Corking Scheme." In order to prevent these creatures from drowning in private swimming pools, he developed a simple method of providing them with permanent floatation by sticking corks onto their prickles. Anyone who is involved with this painstaking task, as thousands are in New Zealand, will understand how it naturally led to a fascination with the sticking on of a variety of other things.

Heather Busch was drawn to an appreciation of the intimate art of the little paper costume by a more aesthetic route. While she is best known for her paintings of extremely old cats, it was an attempt to find new directions in stained glass sculpture that led to her study of the ancient Oriental art of Kokigami. A long time practitioner of body enhancement techniques, she was quick to realise that glass was an inappropriate medium and soon became expert in the design and decoration of lighter and safer paper sculptures. Her work, always tender and radiant with a definite frontal rigidity, now ranks alongside that of Yukiyujo in Japan and Carotte in France.